Instant
SCALE & CHORD GUIDE
for Keyboards

W9-APT-515

Introduction

Key signatures and chord symbols are doors to facility at the keyboard — doors too often locked by insufficient understanding.

This guide unlocks them with clear, simple explanations — additionally providing...

- major and minor scales
- guidelines for scale fingering
- chord charts which include Major, minor, augmented, seventh, ninth, eleventh, major seventh, major ninth, minor seventh, sixth, minor sixth and diminished chords in all positions
- formulas and symbols for altered chords — a simplified approach to forming complex chords
- a glossary of music terms

The easy-to-read text, concise definitions and music illustrations will provide you with an invaluable reference guide in your musical pursuits.

Contents

PART ONE: SCALES AND KEYS
Major Scale Construction

The word **scale** comes from the Latin "scala," which means "ladder." A scale is a ladder of tones. The steps from one tone to the next fall into two categories: 1) the **half step**, which is the distance between two adjacent keys on the keyboard (with no keys in between); and 2) the **whole step**, which equals two half steps. Scales are constructed by a consistent pattern of half steps and whole steps, shown below.

C MAJOR SCALE

This pattern — whole, whole, half, whole, whole, whole, half — can be remembered more easily by dividing the scale into two groups of four notes. Each group has the pattern: whole, whole, half. A whole step separates the four-note groups.

The scale above is a **C** scale because it begins on C. C is called the "keynote," or "tonic." It is a **major** scale because of the interval from the tonic to the third note. An **interval** is simply the distance between two notes. Half steps and whole steps are intervals. The interval from the tonic to the third note of the scale is a **major third** (equal to two whole steps). Thus, the scale is called a major scale.

Each major scale has a **key signature** that reflects the sharps or flats in the scale that arise because of the pattern of whole and half steps. The C major scale has a key signature of no sharps or flat.

Minor Scales

In addition to major scales, there are **minor scales** — scales in which the third note is a **minor third** (one and one-half steps) above the tonic. For every major scale, there is a minor scale with the same key signature, called the **relative minor**. It begins two scale notes below the major scale.

A MINOR SCALE
(relative minor of C major)

This form of the relative minor scale is called the **natural minor**. Another form of the relative minor scale alters the above scale one half step. This form, as given below, is called the **harmonic minor**:

A MINOR SCALE
(harmonic)

The **melodic minor** form of the relative minor scale is created by raising both sixth and seventh notes of the ascending minor scale one half step. The notes for the descending version of this scale return to their natural place, in other words the descending melodic minor scale is identical to the natural minor scale.

The Circle Of Keys

The circle on page 5 illustrates the natural progression of keys at a glance.

- Moving clockwise — by ascending fifths — key signatures increase in the number of sharps (♯).
- Moving counterclockwise — by descending fifths — the key signatures increase in the number of flats (♭).

The keys on the lower part of the circle can be "spelled" either as sharp keys or as flat keys, depending on the direction from which they are approached. This difference in spelling is known as **enharmonic equivalence**, and it applies to individual notes as well as keys; for example, D♯ and E♭ are enharmonically equivalent, as are G♯ and A♭.

Outside the circle are the major keys (uppercase letters) with their relative minors (lowercase letters), and inside are the flats or sharps that form the key signatures.

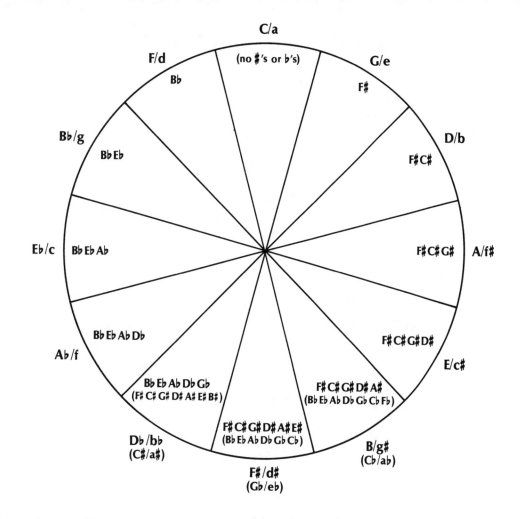

On the following pages you will find a "Directory of Scales and Key Signatures." All of the major and minor scales for the circle of keys are given there.

Knowing what key you're playing in, and knowing the scale of that key, makes playing far easier than regarding the key signature as merely a collection of unrelated sharps or flats. To aid you in learning these scales — and to help you avoid fingering problems encountered in playing music — guideline fingering is given for each hand.

Directory Of Scales And Key Signatures

G Major

G A B C D E F# G F# E D C B A G

E Minor (harmonic)

E F# G A B C D# E D# C B A G F# E

E Minor (melodic)

E F# G A B C# D# E D C B A G F# E

7

9

Cb Major

Cb Db Eb Fb Gb Ab Bb Cb Bb Ab Gb Fb Eb Db Cb

Ab Minor (harmonic)

Ab Bb Cb Db Eb Fb G Ab G Fb Eb Db Cb Bb Ab

Ab Minor (melodic)

Ab Bb Cb Db Eb F G Ab Gb Fb Eb Db Cb Bb Ab

12

F♯ Major

F♯ G♯ A♯ B C♯ D♯ E♯ F♯ E♯ D♯ C♯ B A♯ G♯ F♯

D♯ Minor (harmonic)

D♯ E♯ F♯ G♯ A♯ B C𝄪 D♯ C𝄪 B A♯ G♯ F♯ E♯ D♯

D♯ Minor (melodic)

D♯ E♯ F♯ G♯ A♯ B♯ C𝄪 D♯ C♯ B A♯ G♯ F♯ E♯ D♯

Gb Major

Gb Ab Bb Cb Db Eb F Gb F Eb Db Cb Bb Ab Gb

Eb Minor (harmonic)

Eb F Gb Ab Bb Cb D Eb D Cb Bb Ab Gb F Eb

Eb Minor (melodic)

Eb F Gb Ab Bb C D Eb Db Cb Bb Ab Gb F Eb

C# Major

C# D# E# F# G# A# B# C# B# A# G# F# E# D# C#

A# Minor (harmonic)

A# B# C# D# E# F# G✗ A# G✗ F# E# D# C# B# A#

A# Minor (melodic)

A# B# C# D# E# F✗ G✗ A# G# F# E# D# C# B# A#

15

Db Major

Db Eb F Gb Ab Bb C Db C Bb Ab Gb F Eb Db

Bb Minor (harmonic)

Bb C Db Eb F Gb A Bb A Gb F Eb Db C Bb

Bb Minor (melodic)

Bb C Db Eb F G A Bb Ab Gb F Eb Db C Bb

16

A♭ Major

A♭ B♭ C D♭ E♭ F G A♭ G F E♭ D♭ C B♭ A♭

F Minor (harmonic)

F G A♭ B♭ C D♭ E F E D♭ C B♭ A♭ G F

F Minor (melodic)

F G A♭ B♭ C D E F E♭ D♭ C B♭ A♭ G F

E♭ Major

E♭ F G A♭ B♭ C D E♭ D C B♭ A♭ G F E♭

C Minor (harmonic)

C D E♭ F G A♭ B C B A♭ G F E♭ D C

C Minor (melodic)

C D E♭ F G A B C B♭ A♭ G F E♭ D C

18

20

PART TWO: CHORDS
Basic Chord Construction — Major And Minor Triads

In written music, accompaniment harmony is often indicated by abbreviated **chord symbols** appearing above the staff. This part of the book concerns translating these symbols into notes on the keyboard.

Chords are constructed using intervals of a third, of which there are two kinds: major (equal to two whole steps) and minor (equal to one and one-half steps). The most basic chords are **triads**, which means they consist of three notes.

The note upon which the chord is built is called the **root**; this note gives the chord its letter name. A third above the root is, naturally enough, the **third** of the chord. If the interval from the root to the third is major, it is a major chord; if it is minor, the chord is minor. Another third higher is the **fifth** of the chord, so called because of the interval it forms with the root.

MAJOR

Notice that each kind of triad consists of a major and a minor third, and that the lower of these determines the type of the chord.

MINOR [m, Mi]

Inversions

Of course, the way chords are constructed is not always the way they are used in music. By raising or lowering one or more chord tones by an octave, different chord positions, or **inversions**, are created. While the term "inversion" strictly refers to the use of a chord tone other than the root in the bass, it is applied in a looser sense to keyboard positions regardless of the bass note.

root position   1st inversion   2nd inversion

The chord charts beginning on page 28 show common chords in all inversions, in both treble and bass clef.

The root and fifth are the most common bass notes for major and minor triads, as well as for the higher chord forms which are based on them.

Higher Chord Forms — Major

MAJOR SEVENTH
[maj 7, MA7]

This chord adds a major third above the major triad. The new note is the **major seventh** of the chord, since it lies at the interval of a major seventh above the root.

MAJOR NINTH
[maj 9, MA9]

A minor third added above the major seventh chord. Pianists generally play the root with the left hand, and the remainder of the chord with the right.

SEVENTH [7]

A minor third added above the major triad. Sometimes called a **dominant seventh** chord, since its root is often the fifth note (dominant) of the scale, it tends to lead into the chord on the first note (tonic) of the scale; e.g., C7→F. The remaining major-form chords are dominant chords also.

NINTH [9]

A major third added above the seventh chord. Notice that all notes added above triads alternate major and minor thirds. Distribute the parts as with the major ninth chord.

ELEVENTH [11]

The pure form of this chord adds a minor third above the ninth chord (again, note the alteration of major and minor thirds), but is usually simplified by removing the third of the chord, and sometimes the fifth as well. Distribute the parts as with the major ninth chord. See the sections on Additions And Alterations and Bass Notes Other Than The Root for more about this increasingly popular chord.

THIRTEENTH [13]

A major third above the eleventh chord forms the thirteenth, which is usually reduced as shown, with the third raised an octave. Distribute the parts as with major ninth chords. An alternative is to play a simple seventh chord, since the thirteenth is almost invariably in the melody when this symbol appears.

Higher Chord Forms — Minor

MINOR WITH MAJOR (SHARPED) SEVENTH
[m♯7, m(+7), Mi(MA7)]

Add a major third above the minor triad.

MINOR SEVENTH
[m7, Mi7]

Add a minor third above the minor triad.

MINOR NINTH
[m9, Mi9]

A major third added above the minor seventh chord.

Additions And Alterations

SIXTH [6]

Add the note a whole step above the fifth of the major triad.

MINOR SIXTH [m6, Mi6]

Add a whole step above the fifth of the minor triad.

SIXTH WITH ADDED NINTH [6/9]

A major triad with a sixth and a ninth added.

SEVENTH WITH FLATTED FIFTH [7-9,7(♭9)]

A seventh chord with the fifth lowered one-half step. The flatted fifth can also be considered the root; that is, the notes of C7-5 are enharmonically equivalent to those of G♭7-5.

MINOR SEVENTH WITH FLATTED FIFTH
[m7-5, Mi7(♭5)]

A minor seventh chord with the fifth lowered one-half step. Also called a **half-diminished chord** (see the section on Augmented And Diminished Chords). The third of the chord can be used in the bass, changing it into a minor sixth chord: Cm7-5 = E♭m6.

SEVENTH WITH FLATTED NINTH
[7-9, 7(♭9)]

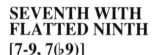

Lower the ninth of the ninth chord one-half step; i.e., add a minor third above a seventh chord.

SEVENTH WITH SHARP NINTH
[7(♯9)]

Raise the ninth of the ninth chord one-half step. The alternate spelling arises out of the use of the sharp ninth as a "blue note," which is a minor third played against a major chord. The fifth of the chord is often omitted.

SUSPENDED FOURTH
[sus, sus4]

Raise the third of a major triad one-half step. The fourth is considered a **suspension** which usually resolves to a third. Seventh chords with a suspended fourth (7sus) are common. Ninth chords with a suspended fourth (9sus) are, for all practical purposes, the same as eleventh chords.

Augmented And Diminished Chords

AUGMENTED
[aug, +]

Raise the fifth of the major triad one-half step. Thus the chord consists of two major thirds. Any of the three chord tones can be considered the root: C+ = E+ = A+. Augmented seventh chords (7+5, +7) are not uncommon.

DIMINISHED (SEVENTH)
[dim, dim 7, °]

This chord consists of three minor thirds. As with the augmented chord, any chord tone is a possible root. Rarely, this symbol calls for the bottom three notes only — a **diminished triad**. A diminished triad with a minor seventh is also common, being called a **half-diminished chord** (ø) or, usually, a **minor seventh chord with flatted fifth** (see Additions And Alterations).

Bass Notes Other Than The Root

The indication of bass notes other than the root, either parenthetically — C(E bass) — or via a "slash" — C/E — generally serves one of two purposes:

- to indicate an important bass line using a certain inversion of a chord; or
- to notate complex chords more simply; e.g., Gm7/C = C11

In connection with the second point, a couple of short cuts will make some complex chords easier to remember:

- For eleventh chords, play the root in the bass and a minor seventh chord on the fifth (Gm7/C), **or** the root in the bass and a major triad on the note a whole step lower (B♭/C).
- For seventh chords with flatted ninth, play the root in the bass and a **diminished** chord on the fifth (Gdim/C), **or**, keeping the root in the bass, play a seventh chord with the root raised one-half step.

C CHORDS

Chord type	Root Position	1st Inversion	2nd Inversion
MAJOR: C	C E G	E G C	G C E
MINOR: Cm CMI	C G (Eb)	Eb G C	G C Eb
AUGMENTED: Caug C+	C E G#	E G# C	G# C E

28

C#/Db CHORDS

C# and Db are enharmonically equivalent. For convenience' sake, all chords have been notated as C# chords.

D CHORDS

Chord type	Root Position	1st Inversion	2nd Inversion

MAJOR:
D

MINOR:
Dm
DMI

AUGMENTED:
Daug
D+

E♭ CHORDS

E CHORDS

F CHORDS

Chord type	Root Position	1st Inversion	2nd Inversion
MAJOR: F			
MINOR: Fm FMI			
AUGMENTED: Faug F+			

Chord type	Root Position	1st Inversion	2nd Inversion	3rd Inversion

F♯/G♭ CHORDS

F♯ and G♭ are enharmonically equivalent. For convenience' sake, all chords have been notated as F♯ chords.

G CHORDS

Chord type	Root Position	1st Inversion	2nd Inversion
MAJOR: G			
MINOR: Gm GMI			
AUGMENTED: Gaug G+			

A♭ CHORDS

A CHORDS

Chord type	Root Position	1st Inversion	2nd Inversion
MAJOR: A			
MINOR: Am Ami			
AUGMENTED: Aaug A+			

B♭ CHORDS

B CHORDS

Chord type	Root Position	1st Inversion	2nd Inversion
MAJOR: B			
MINOR: Bm Bmi			
AUGMENTED: Baug B+			

GLOSSARY

CHORD — Three or more tones played simultaneously. Chords are generally constructed using major and minor thirds.

DOUBLE FLAT (♭♭) — Indicates that a note is to be **lowered a whole step.**

DOUBLE SHARP (x) — Indicates that a note is to be **raised a whole step.**

ENHARMONIC — Notes which are equal in pitch, but different in spelling (e.g. G♯ and A♭).

INTERVAL — The distance in pitch between two tones. The interval is named for the distance between the two note letter names. For example, the interval from A to B is a second (2 letter names), and the interval from A to G is a seventh (7 letter names).

INVERSION — Originally referred to a chord with the third, fifth, or seventh in the bass. More recently, it has come to mean a hand position where the root is not the lowest note, regardless of the true bass note.

KEY — The tonal center of a musical composition. A work is said to be in a certain key if it primarily uses the scale of the same name.

KEY SIGNATURE — The sharps or flats appearing at the beginning of a staff, which show the sharps or flats in the scale of that key.

SCALE — A series of notes arranged in ascending or descending order.

TONIC — The starting note of a scale. Roughly synonymous with key.

TRIAD — A three-note chord.